About Mes

Messy Church® is growing! Every month, families who have never set foot in a church before are enjoying Messy Church, and every month more Messy Churches are started all over the UK and worldwide. Messy Church is proving effective in sharing God's good news with families across denominations and church traditions. We estimate that some 100,000 people belong to Messy Churches—and the number is growing all the time. For more information about Messy Church, visit www.messychurch.org.uk.

Messy Church is enabled, resourced and supported by BRF (Bible Reading Fellowship), a Registered Charity, as one of its core ministries. BRF makes Messy Church freely available and derives no direct income from the work that we do to support it in the UK and abroad.

Would you be willing to support this ministry with your prayer and your giving? To find out more, please visit www.messychurch.org.uk/support-messy-church.

Messy Church® is a registered word mark and the logo is a registered device mark of
The Bible Reading Fellowship

The Bible Reading Fellowship
15 The Chambers, Vineyard
Abingdon OX14 3FE
brf.org.uk

BRF is a Registered Charity (223280)

ISBN 978 1 84101 824 9
First published 2011; reprinted 2012, 2013, 2016
10 9 8 7 6 5 4 3
All rights reserved

Acknowledgments
Unless otherwise stated, scripture quotations are taken from the Contemporary English Version
of the Bible published by HarperCollins Publishers, copyright © 1991, 1992, 1995 American Bible
Society.

Page 29: Scripture quotations taken from The Holy Bible, New International Version (Anglicised
edition) copyright © 1979, 1984, 2011 by Biblica. Used by permission of Hodder & Stoughton
Publishers, a Hachette UK company. All rights reserved. 'NIV' is a registered trademark of Biblica.
UK trademark number 1448790.

A catalogue record for this book is available from the British Library

Printed and bound by CPI Group (UK) Ltd, Croydon CR0 4YY

Lucy Moore

For Hannah and William Fisher, Elizabeth Harley
and Murray Bean, who have exerted so much effort
and skill to interest me in sport to so little effect

Thanks to Martyn Payne, Charis Lambert,
Bob Morris and my imaginative family
for all your help and inspiration

Contents

Foreword 7

Introduction 9

One-off community family events 12
Messy sports trail 12
Virtual torch relay 15
Messy water sports 15
Round the world safari meal 16
Messy 'get healthy' programme 17
Messy gym 19
Messy family weekend 19
Messy family Grand Prix 19
Wii Fit family fun 19
Healthy eating cookathon 20

Messy Church sports session 21

Sports-related crafts 27

Sports-related activities 29
Bible verse praise 29
Energetic Bible journeys 31
Redeeming football chants 33
Mime, dance, movement 33

Sports-related Messy Church celebrations 34
Theme: Excellence 34
Theme: Friendship 36
Theme: Respect 39
Theme: Everyone's valuable 42

Active all-age games from around the world 47
New Zealand 47
Israel 47
Ghana 48
Pakistan 49
China 49
Caribbean islands 49
Nigeria 50
Indonesia 50
North America 50
Brazil 51

Healthy eating from around the world 52

Active prayers 54
Ball prayers 54
Popping prayers 54
Goal prayers 55
Jesus Prayer jogging 56
Relay prayer 57
Picture prayer 58

Foreword

Ask the children and adults at Messy Church about glue and I'm sure they will tell you that it feels good, it can be a bit messy, but it's mostly fun and it does its job well: it binds and it fixes.

Sport is like glue. It too feels good, it can sometimes be a bit messy, but it's mostly fun and it does its job extremely well because it binds people together and fixes memories.

What is it that makes sport such effective human glue? What is its formula? When we take part in sport we give attention to each other by making time for one another. Sport also compels us to communicate; we talk and smile and laugh together—and not just while we are taking part in a sporting activity, but for days, weeks and even years to follow as we recall the shared memories of an amusing or momentous incident. The effects of it can still be seen long after the glue has dried.

But sport has a secret ingredient too. It's something that, for many, is harder to identify, but it's the best part of the recipe because it's the element that makes our spirits soar. The secret ingredient is God. He has designed people for sport and designed sport for people—and as our bodies move and our hearts pump, he refreshes our souls.

Sport can be worship, and where better to enjoy the gift of sport than at a Messy Church? We are united as families, all ages and all abilities moving together, talking together, laughing together and, in doing so, worshipping together the God who designed us and created us.

Lucy has filled this book with original, inspirational and fun sporting ideas. The creativity with which God has blessed her brims from every page. And so as Lucy has shared with us, let us—in turn—share these ideas with the families who come along to Messy Church. As we do so, we will deepen relationships and bring people closer to their creator. This is why I am convinced that Messy Church and sport is truly a match made in heaven.

MARK CHESTER, AUTHOR OF *THE SOUL OF FOOTBALL* (BRF, 2015)

Introduction

We all know that exercise is good for our health, games can bring people together, disciplined training can be character-building and very few of us do a sensible amount of exercise, either of body or of soul. In church we follow Jesus, who came to bring life in all its fullness and who spent much of his time making people physically healthy as well as spiritually healthy. We therefore have a responsibility to encourage all sorts of wellbeing in the people we serve.

A major sporting event of any kind is an opportunity to focus on this wellbeing among the families who enjoy Messy Church, and can even be an occasion that encourages members of the family who haven't yet come and joined in to give Messy Church a try. Whether it's the Olympics, the World Cup, the Ashes or Wimbledon, there is usually a sporting event happening that can provide a reason to focus a Messy Church session on sport or to put on an extra sports-related community family event.

There are plenty of opportunities for individuals of different ages and abilities to be sporty in segregated groups, but Messy Church is all about getting different people together: people of different ages, with different abilities, in different family situations. So the sport-related activities in this book try to be as inclusive of all ages and abilities as possible. They are suggested in the spirit of bringing whole families and communities together to enjoy themselves and to find out how brilliant different people are in different ways. There are some elements of competition for those who enjoy competing, some elements of creativity for those who like constructing, and some elements of healthy eating, healthy spirituality and healthy 'being' for those interested in the holistic nature of health; that wholeness which is sometimes called 'shalom'.

Another theme running through the book is that of enjoying the international element of sport. With competitors coming together from all over the world, sporting events are a good time to think about other cultures—their flags, their languages, their games, and their foods.

It's worth mentioning that not all agree that competitiveness is to be prized. While some people enjoy competing, in many sports there can only be one winner amid many runners-up. Family is all about helping every member to grow, so the activities in this book include more activities that don't have runners-up than ones in which there is only one winner. (Although there are a few for those who do find competition fun.)

You may wish to pick and mix from the whole book and use all sorts of different activities for your particular event. It's just a starting block to encourage you to think about the possibilities in your community for making the most of a national emphasis on sport in the media at a particular time.

As with any Messy Church, the spiritual value will come even more from the commitment, relationships, awareness and understanding of the people running it than from the content of the events themselves. Team training has never been so important!

LUCY MOORE

One-off community family events

Messy sports trail

This is an excuse to get the whole family out in the local park, wood or open space doing mild exercise but mainly having fun together. You could also hold this event inside, in a sports hall or church building.

Select ten stations at roughly equal distances from each other. Try to use a route and sports that are accessible for all ages and all abilities, including people with disabilities. At each station post two or more team leaders with an activity.

At each station you will need: high-visibility jackets (one per helper), a drinking water supply, first-aid kit, mobile phone, score sheet (optional), stopwatch, simple passport made from folded card (one per family), stamp and inkpad for the passports.

You will need Public Liability Insurance and permission to use the land. (Your local council should be able to advise you.)

You'll also need to have a risk assessment and to make clear to families on the publicity material that they are responsible for their children. People also need to be aware of any hazards you foresee, such as messiness, uneven ground, unsuitable footwear, need for water, insect bite cream, sun cream and so on.

Each family is given a passport that they get stamped at each station to show that they have attempted the activity. If you're running the event as a competition, you'll need to time or measure each family's achievement and record it. Either way, make sure everyone gets a medal or prize of some sort.

The activities are suggested on the assumption that you don't have access to qualified coaches and equipment, but, if you do, you will no doubt wish to make use of them!

Sports trail activities

- Transporting as much water as possible in a spoon held between your teeth (or in your hand if you want to break people in gently)
- Balloon badminton or volleyball
- Archery with foam-tipped or suction pad arrows
- Time taken to eat a strung-up doughnut without using your hands
- Skittles
- Pétanque
- Football goal scoring (using hands or feet)
- Building a boat to sail across a paddling pool, powered by water shot from a water pistol
- Building the highest tower in a set time out of marshmallows and uncooked spaghetti
- Water-balloon throwing
- Hula hoop: who can hula the longest

- Paper-plate discus: throw or flip a paper plate as far as possible
- Cocktail-stick javelin
- Blowing the most bubbles through an opening
- Human noughts and crosses: the first team to have three members sitting in a straight line on chairs set out in a three-by-three square
- Cross-country skiing: in advance, drill four holes at regular distances along two planks and thread cords through them. Four members of a team place one foot on each plank, hold the cords taut and try to cover a short distance in as short a time as possible whilst keeping their feet on the planks.

Slightly messier activities

- Apple bobbing
- Wet slide: how far can you slide down the wet tarpaulin? (Protective clothing will be needed.)
- Hand to mouth: in a dustbin bag for two, with one person behind the other, one person feeds the other
- Fishing out alphabet pasta letters to make words
- Taking sweets out of mashed jelly using only your teeth
- Carrying water in a leaky bucket in relays to fill a container
- Throwing wet sponges at someone in the stocks with points for hitting different parts of them.

N.B. Any website with 'games for your youth group' will have many really messy activities to choose from.

Virtual torch relay

Start the ball rolling by getting one person to email an image of an Olympic torch to another person in the congregation or community with a simple message attached inviting that person to send it to two other contacts in the area. Those two people each send it to two of their own local contacts, and so on. Ask for the people who receive the email to copy in the senders when forwarding it so that you can keep a tally of how many people you manage to email before the deadline. You could include an invitation to see an actual torch burning at a picnic, sports afternoon or other event you're organising locally.

Messy water sports

Devise family-friendly water sports on a beach, or in a garden with all the paddling pools and baby baths you can get your hands on. Make sure that families are fully aware that they are responsible for the safety of their own children and that they need to take all necessary precautions to avoid accidents. Conclude the event with a barbecue.

All-age, all-ability adaptations of the water sports could include:

- Diving: pick up objects from the bottom of the pool by dipping in your hands. (Participants are given blindfolds to wear.)
- Swimming: travel down a water slide made from a long sheet of tarpaulin (drenched with a hosepipe)
- Synchronised swimming: with one person in each paddling pool, videoed from above
- Canoe or kayak sprint: compete with wind-up boats or use bath toys
- Canoe or kayak slalom: compete with radio-controlled boats
- Beach volleyball: use a large, lightweight beach ball
- Sailing: build and race homemade rafts and award prizes for speed and style
- Rowing: propel a wheelchair across land with oars with a child on your lap to 'help'.

Round the world safari meal

Organise a family safari meal with a global theme. You need different houses to host each course of the meal and the whole group walks together from house to house between courses after helping with the washing up. You could invite the hosts to plan their course with healthy eating and with the theme of a particular country. At each home, a family game could be played from the country represented (see **Active all-age games from around the world**, pages 47–51, for ideas). You might want different people to organise the games each time to save the host having to do everything. On a larger scale, you could organise a safari meal between Messy Churches in your area and travel by bike, car or bus.

Messy 'get healthy' programme

Hold a 'get healthy' month. Each day for one month, invite families to try to achieve one manageable challenge that will exercise body, mind or spirit without taking too long or costing much.

- Day 1: run past five lamp posts
- Day 2: be kind to one person
- Day 3: try a fruit you've never eaten before
- Day 4: have an arm-wrestling competition
- Day 5: sit for two minutes in silence round a candle
- Day 6: phone someone and cheer them up
- Day 7: go for a walk together
- Day 8: drink an extra glass of water
- Day 9: ask one unanswerable question
- Day 10: climb a suitable tree and take a photo of each other in it
- Day 11: say a prayer for someone who is unwell
- Day 12: do ten star jumps
- Day 13: walk to your local church and decide which is your favourite part of it

- Day 14: listen to a piece of music chosen by the youngest member of the family
- Day 15: do one thing for another person without expecting any reward
- Day 16: say thank you to God for the meal you share
- Day 17: give something away
- Day 18: bake biscuits together
- Day 19: put on some lively music and dance for one whole track
- Day 20: do something you've never done before
- Day 21: say a goodnight prayer at bedtime
- Day 22: do 20 press-ups or sit-ups
- Day 23: listen to a piece of music chosen by the oldest member of the family
- Day 24: say hello to everyone you meet
- Day 25: say what the most mysterious thing in the universe is
- Day 26: learn how to say hello in a foreign language
- Day 27: tell each other your favourite Bible stories
- Day 28: invite someone to choose their favourite picture and ask everyone to listen while they explain why they like it
- Day 29: do the conga round every room in the house
- Day 30: play indoor skittles
- Day 31: buy a skipping rope and challenge each other to personal bests.

Messy gym

Negotiate with your local gym, swimming pool, dance or sports centre to hold a family event there.

Messy family weekend

Have a whole messy family weekend camp on a healthy living theme, including fun sports, dancing, celebration, construction and lots of food and drink.

Messy family Grand Prix

Hold a family-friendly fundraising race with entrance fees and sponsorship going to a worthy cause. Invite family teams to take part together to go round a manageable course on whatever vehicles they like: scooters, rollerblades, tricycles, pushchairs, wheelchairs, shopmobility scooters, pogo sticks, and so on. Encourage fancy dress or team colours.

Wii Fit family fun

Get your hands on as many Wii Fit machines as you can and arrange a circuit so that each family can have a short time on each machine. Persuade your teenagers to compile a set of funny YouTube clips of sporting events to watch together at the end over fruit juice and wholewheat snacks.

Healthy eating cookathon

Hold a family cooking session to make a healthy, tasty meal on a tight budget and, of course, eat the resulting meal together.

Messy Church sports session: The good Samaritan

The parable of the good Samaritan comes in the context of a discussion about striving for excellence, about what rules to keep, and about our relationship with God and with those around us. All these are sporty themes as well as spiritual ones, making it a highly suitable subject for a Messy Church session on sport.

Craft ideas

- Wrap a friend or family member in bandages or toilet paper
- The good Samaritan treated the man's wounds with olive oil and with wine—decorate little glass or plastic bottles of olive oil
- Make wine-bottle candleholders by dribbling an empty wine bottle with warm wax (adult supervision needed) and making a bead necklace to decorate it
- Draw round your hands to decorate a card to give to someone telling them how kind they are
- Make donkeys out of cardboard boxes. Open up a cardboard box and fold the flaps of the base up or down so that you can stand inside the resultant hollow rectangle made up of the four vertical sides.

Pull it up to your middle so that it looks as if you are riding the donkey. Make two straps that are stapled or sticky-taped on to the box and are long enough to go over the shoulders.

- Draw traffic signs to colour in: what stops us helping others? What makes us deviate from being a good neighbour? What hazards are ahead?
- Pray about those people we find hard to love. Write their name, or draw a picture of them, on an acetate or Perspex heart. Drop on olive oil as a sign of healing and wrap the heart in a bandage as a sign of care. Let's not make excuses like the priest and Levite did: Jesus calls us to love each other simply and unconditionally. Repeat this exercise with your own name: God knows we can all be hard to love, but he treasures each one of us whatever we're like.
- Make invitations using calligraphy for a dinner4good. See www.dinner4good.com for details.
- Make a first-aid box and fill it with basic first-aid equipment. Add cardboard crosses to give to people whose feelings are hurt. The crosses should be blank on one side to decorate and have a verse on the other side.
- Make a story bracelet with beads of different colours and shapes to tell the story. Three hearts for the love of God, neighbour and self; rectangle for a road; triangle for the mountains; doughnut shape for a robbers' cave; star or jagged shape for robbers fighting; red for blood; blue for the priest; green for the Levite; yellow for the Samaritan; bottle shape for

oil or wine; pony bead for the donkey; square for the inn; silver circles for coins; a further heart shape for 'go and do the same'.

- Make a sand scene using a sand tray and toy people to tell or act out the story
- Cut out pictures from magazines and make a 'who is my neighbour?' collage. Try to find people of different ages, races and genders. Alternatively, invite people to draw a picture of themselves in one house and pictures of others in the next-door house.

Celebration

Introduce the idea of celebrating the Olympic Games (or another major sporting event). Ask people what their favourite sport is. Say that sporting events are all about people doing their very best.

Arrange for some volunteers to be in sports kit to play the parts in the story below. If possible, read the story as if you were a sports commentator. Invite those in sports kit to improvise sports, making the mime as funny as they can.

There was once a man who asked Jesus how he could be the best. Not how he could win a gold medal or a football trophy, but how he could win what mattered most to him. 'Good teacher,' he said, 'how can I win eternal life?' He knew he should love God and love his neighbour, but then he asked Jesus, 'Who is my neighbour?' And Jesus replied with a story. Perhaps a modern-day version might be a little bit like this:

'Well, here we are on the track between Jerusalem and Jericho and we're here to see some fantastic athletes in action today. There they are, all warming up as you can see. What an amazing bunch they are! Let's give them a cheer!

First off, it's the men's 3000 metre hurdles, and here's our man from [insert your national team name], running down this very rugged mountain path now. Yes! He's jumped the roadblock signs. Oooh, and he's hurdled over the mountain goat! And there he goes over a large boulder... But what's this? Oh dear, I think he's ended up in the middle of the Taekwondo... and the judo... and, oh dear, is that the boxing team? And surely not the archery team? And what are the javelin throwers doing here? Or the hammer throwers? Or the rapid-fire pistol team? And the wrestlers? These boys are big... ouch!... and brutal... ouch! They've made mincemeat of our poor team member. I'm sure they're not supposed to take all his clothes with them when they run off... And surely they shouldn't leave him bleeding all over the road like that?

But never mind! Here comes another of our team. It's one of the captains! He's going to look after his team member, I'm quite sure... and he's coming up to our injured man now... and he's slowing down... he's stopping... and what's this? He's sprinting away at full speed! What a turn of speed! What acceleration! Perhaps he thinks it's against the rules to stop and help in the middle of a race? He's going to manage that sprint in record time! Which means medals for him, but what about our poor injured man? Is he out of the race for good?

Ah, good, another of our team captains is coming down the road. Our man will be fine now. He's coming nearer... and nearer... oooh, watch these mental gymnastics as he wrestles with his conscience! And my word, what a magnificent triple jump he does to get as far away as possible when he sees what a mess that man is!

But who's this coming now? Oh no, it's one of the [fill in whichever nationality is the major competitor at the moment] team! What's he doing? He's stopping! He's going over to our man... he's sponging him down! He's giving him oranges! He must be a weightlifter! Look at him lifting him up... and yes! They're off down the road, and now they're in the lead... they're coming up to the finishing line and... they've won this year's steeplechase! This is amazing! Our enemy is our friend! This makes no sense at all! Let's hear it for the man from [opposing team name]!'

And Jesus said, 'Which of these men was a neighbour to the man who had been attacked?' Of course it was the one who helped him. Nothing was going to get in the way of the man from [opposing team name] helping that injured man—not race, religion, or rules of any sort. So if we want to win the best medal of all—the prize of pleasing God—it's very easy! We just have to love God and love our neighbour, and look after other people around us, no matter what everyone else thinks we should do.

Prayer

Sports spectators do a lot of cheering. Invite everyone to join in the following prayer with a big 'Yeeeeah!' (or 'whoop' or 'hooray' or whatever cheering noise you like best).

Jesus, you are the greatest champion of all (cheer!)
You tell fantastic stories (cheer!)
We want to be the best people we can be for you and for each other (cheer!)
Please help us to remember you every minute of every day (cheer!)
And to put other people first, especially those we don't like (cheer!)
Jesus, you really are the best! (cheer!)

Sports-related crafts

Sports crafts give opportunities to talk about teamwork, looking after everyone in a team, supportive roles, striving for excellence, persistence, the ultimate prize, the culture of other countries, making a joyful noise and similar sporty spiritual themes. Search the internet or craft books for instructions to make or extend the following ideas as needed.

- Flags
- Rosettes
- Medals
- Olympic wreaths
- Food from different countries
- Decorated T-shirts, caps, go-faster socks, drinking bottles, and so on
- Vuvuzelas or rattles
- Cheerleaders' pom-poms
- Streamers for the 'opening ceremony'
- Equipment for active games such as cardboard hoops for quoits, bases for limbo pole support, boxes cut with numbered tunnels for marble rolling, Gogoim boxes (see **Active all-age games from around the world**, pages 47–51)
- Skittles from plastic bottles
- Friendship bracelets
- Kicking a football in paint over a large sheet of paper

- Bouncing a ping-pong ball or tennis ball in paint over a large sheet of paper
- Roller-skating or skateboarding in paint
- Drawing faces on hexagons (like those on footballs) and fitting them together as a mosaic around a ball or balloon
- Making a huge crowd cheering on competitors (links to the 'large crowd of witnesses' in Hebrews 12:1)
- Colouring in a large picture in a given length of time until someone takes over (as in a relay race)
- Making healthy eating snacks
- Making a marble run from cardboard tubes and seeing whose marble comes out fastest
- Making energy drink cocktails
- Making a life plan: decorate and use stickers to mark achievements
- Inviting a life coach (or vicar) to talk through your life plan
- Holding trebuchet-style competitions by making a contraption to fire a missile or small doll over a high or long distance
- Designing a sporty outfit for a doll or a friend from scraps of material or newspaper.

Sports-related activities

Bible verse praise

Choose one of the Bible passages below involving different extremities, or pick your own.

How wide and long and high and deep is the love of Christ.

EPHESIANS 3:18, NIV

If I go up to the heavens, you are there; if I make my bed in the depths, you are there.

PSALM 139:8, NIV

Can you understand the mysteries surrounding God All-Powerful? They are higher than the heavens and deeper than the grave. So what can you do when you know so little, and these mysteries outreach the earth and the sea?

JOB 11:7–9

Your love reaches higher than the heavens, and your loyalty extends beyond the clouds.

PSALM 108:4

Just as the heavens are higher than the earth, my thoughts and my ways are higher than yours.

ISAIAH 55:9

He drags strong rulers from their thrones and puts humble people in places of power.
LUKE 1:52

Design a 'fitness praise trail' based on one or more of the passages above to combine praise and actions. You might have four or five stations around a circuit with the praise verse repeated at each one. For example:

How wide *(stretch out to either side as far as you can)* … and long *(lie down on your front and stretch out as much as you can)* … and high *(stand up and reach up as high as you can)* … and deep *(bend over and touch your toes)* … is the love of Christ *(make a large circle shape with your arms)*.

Move to the next point and repeat the series of words and movements.

Alternatively, you could have a different passage and set of actions to learn at each station and treat it as circuit training, with a set time to continue at each station before a whistle blows and everyone moves on to the next station. The competitive among you could keep a tally of how many times they manage to carry out the sequence at each station.

Energetic Bible journeys

Choose the story of a Bible journey and tell it energetically. (See the example below.) The emphasis in this activity is more on movement than on a deep appreciation of the story's meaning. The idea is simply to tell the story using the different points in it to inspire actions, exercise or movement. If you can, tell it very fast in a very large space and move around it as widely as possible. If this is not possible, running on the spot is a good alternative.

Philip and the Ethiopian official

ACTS 8:1–8, 26–40

The people who first believed in Jesus were all together in Jerusalem. But Stephen was stoned to death for believing in Jesus. And on that day many believers had to run for their lives.

They ran to Judea (*run a long way north*)
… and Samaria (*run further north*)
… They told people about Jesus wherever they went (*pass round a fast Chinese whisper of 'Have you heard about Jesus?'*).

Philip went down to a city in Samaria (*walk east a little way*)
… and told people about Jesus (*pass round a fast Chinese whisper of 'Have you heard about Jesus?'*).

Crowds of people wanted to belong to Jesus, so Philip took them down to the river *(walk west a little way)*
… and baptised them to show they belonged to Jesus *('swim' fast in a circle)*.

Then an angel said to Philip, 'Go south to the desert road that goes down from Jerusalem to Gaza.' So he started out *(walk south)*
… and on his way he met a man from Ethiopia who was an important official in charge of all the queen's treasure. This man had gone to Jerusalem to worship and, on his way home, was sitting in his chariot reading the book of the prophet Isaiah. The Holy Spirit told Philip to catch up with the chariot.

So Philip ran up to the chariot *(run south very fast and keep running)*
… and heard the man reading from the book of the prophet Isaiah.

'Do you understand what you are reading?' Philip asked. The official answered, 'How can I understand unless someone helps me?'

He then invited Philip to come up and sit beside him *(crouch down and bounce on the ground—keep bouncing)*.

Philip began with the very passage of scripture the man was reading and told him the good news about Jesus. As they travelled along the road, they came to some water and the Ethiopian said, 'Look! Here is water. Why can't I be baptised?' He ordered the chariot to stop *(stop bouncing)*.

Then both Philip and the Ethiopian official went down into the water *(walk east a little way)*
... and Philip baptised him *(swim round in a circle)*.

When they came up out of the water, the Holy Spirit suddenly took Philip away to Azotus *(fly jet-aeroplane-like south)*
... and he travelled about, talking about Jesus in all the towns until he reached Caesarea *(run north a long way—further than Samaria—in a zigzag, saying, 'Have you heard about Jesus?' repeatedly as you go)*.

Redeeming football chants

Take the catchy rhythm of a well-known football or rugby chant and replace the words with words of praise to God. (It's best to avoid those with unsuitable words.) For example, 'You're not singing any more' becomes 'I'll be singing evermore'; 'Play up Pompey' becomes 'Praise God always' or 'Rejoice always', and so on.

Mime, dance, movement

Instead of depending on words, use mime, dance and movement to communicate a story such as creation, Christmas, or Holy Week and Easter.

Sports-related Messy Church celebrations

The celebration ideas below include a story or talk and a prayer suggestion. They are based on Olympic values or around sporty themes in general, and are designed to draw out Christian themes. If you wish to add music, use resources you have at your disposal to include songs familiar to your Messy Church families.

Theme: Excellence

Introduction

If sports people want to be the best they possibly can be, they need to be fit in body, mind and spirit. A sports player might be determined to win, but they won't achieve their best if they smoke 50 cigarettes a day or eat chips for breakfast. Equally, it is no use doing six hours of training per day but spending the whole time worrying or being frightened inside. Sports champions need to be fit in their bodies and their minds. If we want to become the best people we can be, we will benefit from a healthy combination of a strong mind, body and spirit. Jesus knows how important it is to be whole on the inside and on the outside. He doesn't just care about making bodies well; he also cares about people's minds and spirits.

Tell the story of the paralysed man let down through the roof (Luke 5:17–26), and then ask the following questions.

- How might the man have felt when Jesus said that his sins were forgiven?
- Why didn't Jesus just make his legs better?
- Which was more important to the man: to be forgiven or to walk again?
- Which was more important to his friends? Or to the crowd?
- What does this story make you think about Jesus?

Prayer

Invite everyone to think of someone who is unwell or unhappy and to place a paper cut-out figure on a mat to represent that person. Together, carry the mat to a cross and put it gently down in front of it. A suggested prayer might be:

Lord Jesus, we bring you all these friends of ours who are hurting in some way, and we ask you to make them whole again, so that they can enjoy the full life that you want for them. Amen

Theme: Friendship

Introduction

Sport is a great way for people to make friends, however different they are. Think of sportsmen and women who are good friends even though they're competitors (for example, Roger Federer and Rafael Nadal). Real friends can go to great lengths to try to understand each other, because they care deep down about each other. Sometimes they even fight until they've got their problems straightened out! I wonder if any wrestlers are friends? (If there's time, you could have an arm-wrestling or thumb wars match at this point.) Many years ago, there were two wrestlers who became very good friends.

Tell the following story, using images from the internet to accompany the storytelling if possible. The story can be found in Genesis 32:22–32.

Jacob wasn't sure if God was his friend or not. God was friends with his parents, but Jacob wasn't sure if God was definitely friends with him too. Perhaps some of us are like that: we know our mum or dad or nan or grandpa is friends with God, but we don't know if we are friends with God too.

Jacob was out in the desert all on his own one night, with his family life—as usual—in a real mess. Suddenly, someone came up to him in the dark and started fighting with him! Jacob wasn't going to take that sitting down, so he fought back. They wrestled and they struggled and they grappled with each other until it was nearly dawn. Sometimes when we're fighting or arguing with someone, even if we don't agree with them at all, we can find ourselves really admiring the way they are arguing or fighting. Jacob and the stranger got to know each other better with every half nelson. And they liked each other more and more. The stranger caught Jacob on the hip so that it popped out of its socket, but Jacob was so determined that he just kept on fighting, even though it really, really hurt. Eventually, the stranger gasped, 'Let go of me! It's nearly daylight!' Now Jacob thought he might know who this mysterious stranger was, so he panted, 'I'm not going to let you go until you bless me.'

'What's your name?' breathed the stranger, wriggling to try to get away from Jacob.

'Jacob!' wheezed Jacob, pressing down harder.

'Not any more!' said the stranger. 'You've wrestled with God and with people and you've won. So your name will be Israel, which means "He wrestles with God".'

Jacob (or rather, Israel) said, 'Now you tell me your name.'

'Don't you know who I am?' said the stranger. And he blessed Jacob (or Israel) and disappeared. And Jacob (or Israel) knew who it was.

'Wow,' thought Jacob (or Israel). 'I've seen God face to face and I'm still alive!'

That struggle with God didn't just help Jacob to see God as his own friend; it helped Jacob see his family in a new way too.

Perhaps sometimes we should be ready to 'wrestle' with God, especially if we want our friendship with him to grow. It might not be wrestling in the way that Jacob wrestled, but it might be not letting go of God until he's given us an answer to a prayer, or a word of guidance, or until we're sure we have his blessing.

Prayer

Have some of the following questions printed out onto separate cards. Include others that you think your families might be asking God.

- Do you exist?
- Did you make the world?
- Why do bad things happen to good people?
- Why don't you make wars stop?
- What are your plans for me?
- How do I know you're there?
- How do I know you love me?
- How should I be living my life?
- Is the Bible true?

Rig up a boxing or wrestling ring with some rope and invite everyone to talk about the questions on the cards and then choose one which they think it would be worth wrestling with God about. Invite them to place their cards in the ring, asking God to help them be friends as they wrestle with this question.

Conclude the prayers with a word of thanks to God for always wanting to go further with us, even if we've known him for years.

You might like to have available some books or leaflets on Christian basics, flyers for the next Alpha course, or simply someone available to help people start their 'wrestling' with some informed answers or further questions.

Theme: Respect

Introduction

Respecting others in sport really makes sense. If, for example, competitors didn't respect the rules, how could they possibly compete? Arrange for some volunteers to do simple, silly dramas such as the ones below.

- Someone shouting, 'I won the cycling!' and someone else saying, 'But you were riding a motorbike!' (This would also work with kayaking using a motorboat, pole vaulting using a trampoline… and so on.)
- Someone tying their competitor's shoelaces together before the start of the race and laughing when they fall over
- Someone starting a race just in front of the finishing line
- Someone carrying an arrow to the target and sticking it by hand into the centre.

We need rules to help things work smoothly and to make sure everyone has a fair chance. In the Bible, God gave his people rules to live by that still work today: to protect people, to give them the best way to live together in society, and to give everyone, especially those who are needy and defenceless, a fair chance. Once everybody used to know these rules off by heart, but nowadays we need to be reminded of them.

Tell the story of the Ten Commandments using the idea below or sourcing the story from:

either: Godly Play: The ten best ways to live, which can be found in *The Complete Guide to Godly Play Volume 2* by Jerome W. Berryman (Living the Good News, 2002)

or: Barnabas in Churches website: Ten commandments by Martyn Payne (go to www.barnabasinchurches.org. uk/ten-commandments).

The Ten Commandments

In the Bible, God wanted his people to have the very best life possible and to shine out as an example to all those who didn't know how well life works when you follow God. So he spent a long time building a relationship with them, rescuing them from Egypt, leading them through all sorts of dangers and showing them how much they could trust him. He gave them ten rules to help them know how best to live (see Exodus 20:1–17).

Display and read out the Ten Commandments using different people's voices. Try to learn them together by using one of the following methods or one of your own. The idea is for everyone to become familiar with the Ten Commandments.

- Put shortened versions of each commandment on balloons and gradually pop the balloons, seeing if people can still remember them all as the balloons are popped.
- Divide into groups and give out sets of the commandments to each group. (Use symbols as well as words for those who can't read.) See which group is the first to hold up a commandment that's about: respecting marriage; respecting language; respecting the truth; respecting God; respecting life; respecting members of your family; respecting people around you; respecting other people's things; respecting what you own; respecting your body clock; respecting yourself.
- Give each person a card with a commandment written on it in words and symbols and ask them to run to the front if their commandment is about the topics you shout out.

Prayer

Jesus came to write God's rules not on stones but on our hearts so that, rather than just feeling we had to keep them, we would really want to keep them. Read out the Ten Commandments one by one and invite everyone to respond with the word 'respect' if they think it is a good way to live. If they don't agree with it, or they're not sure yet, invite them to ask God quietly in their own heart to show them over the next month what he means by that commandment.

Theme: Everyone's valuable

Introduction

Sporting competitions show us people who are truly excellent at their chosen sports, but they also demonstrate how valuable every single person is.

Each competitor has a team behind them: coaches, physiotherapists, parents, friends, sponsors, and so on. Nobody can do it on their own. Many international sports events also celebrate people with disabilities and the way they overcome them. We can all enjoy cheering on our teams at a sports event or on TV—the teams appreciate our support just as we appreciate their excellence. We are all connected. When things work properly, nobody is pretending to be somebody they're not; everyone is being themselves, doing their own job to the best of their ability.

In the Bible, we read that, at its best, church is like that. The apostle Paul wrote a letter explaining that the church was like a healthy body (1 Corinthians 12:12–27). Tell the story using the version below, or the final track of the *Messy Church* DVD. The reflective story below was first used on a parish weekend with the theme 'unity in Christ'. The passage from 1 Corinthians 12:12–27 is familiar to many. However, turning the words into something concrete and visible, as this story does, gives people a chance to engage with it more directly and hear what God is saying to them about their own feelings with regard to their part in the body of Christ. For the storytelling, invite everyone to sit in a semicircle in front of you. The biblical text is taken from the Contemporary English Version. There is a retelling in *The Barnabas Children's Bible*, story 344 (Barnabas, 2007).

You will need: a piece of felt to act as a backcloth on which to lay the body parts for the story; some body parts cut from art foam or card (feet, hands, head, main body part, arms, legs, some internal organs, large eye, large ear, underwear).

One body with many parts

(Place the backcloth on the floor in front of you.)

The body of Christ has many different parts, just as any other body does.

(Place all the body parts jumbled up on to the backcloth.)

Our bodies don't have just one part. They have many parts.

(Pick up a foot.)

Suppose a foot says, 'I'm not a hand, and so I'm not part of the body.' Wouldn't the foot still belong to the body?

(Pick up an ear.)

Or suppose an ear says, 'I'm not an eye, and so I'm not part of the body.' Wouldn't the ear still belong to the body?

(Place a large eye over the body.)

If our bodies were only an eye, we couldn't hear a thing.

(Place a large ear over the body.)

And if they were only an ear, we couldn't smell a thing.

(Sort the body parts to make a body on the backcloth.)

But God has put all the parts of our body together in the way that he decided is best. A body isn't really a body, unless there is more than one part. It takes many parts to make a single body.

(Temporarily remove the hands and then replace them.)

That's why the eyes cannot say they don't need the hands.

(Temporarily remove the feet, replace them and then add internal organs.)

In fact, we cannot get along without the parts of the body that seem to be the weakest.

(Place underwear over the groin area.)

We take special care to dress up some parts of our bodies. We are modest about some parts, but we don't have to be modest about other parts.

(Run your fingers over the body on the backcloth.)

God put our bodies together in such a way that even the parts that seem the least important are valuable. He did this to make all parts of the body work together smoothly, with each part caring about the others. If one part of our body hurts, we hurt all over. If one part of our body is honoured, the whole body will be happy.

(Look up and indicate everyone in the circle.)

Together we are the body of Christ. Each one of us is part of his body.

(Pause and then ask some open-ended questions, reflecting on which part of the storytelling people liked the best, which part is important for them at the moment, and so on.)

Prayer

Sketch out with your hands a large body shape on the floor. Invite everyone to go and stand in the shape according to which part they think they are in the body of Christ. Ask them to say why they have chosen that particular part. For example, 'I'm a hand because I'm always helping other people'; 'I'm a bowel because nobody sees the important work I do.' When everyone is in place, do a 'roll call' of all the different parts of the body to include everyone and then hold hands together and say, 'Together we are the body of Christ!'

Active all-age games from around the world

New Zealand: Hei Tama Tu Tama

This is an active version of the 'stone, scissors, paper' game, and looks a little like the Maori haka dance. There are four possible positions: hands on hips; the left hand held up as a fist and the other on a hip; the right hand as a fist and the other on a hip; both hands up in the air as fists.

Two players stand facing each other. One of the players calls out, 'One Hei Tama Tu Tama', and on the final word, both players simultaneously choose one of the positions. If they mirror each other (for example, the caller has right fist up and the challenger has left fist up), the caller wins a point and continues with the next round, this time saying 'Two Hei Tama Tu Tama'. If they are different positions, nobody wins a point and the challenger becomes the caller and calls the next round. The winner is the first to get to 'Ten Hei Tama Tu Tama'. Only the caller can win a point.

Israel: Gogoim

This game is traditionally played with apricot pits, but can be played with any small missiles. To keep the fruity theme you could use olive pits, plum stones, acorns, conkers or cherry pits, or you could make a larger version with bean bags, or use counters.

Make a target box for each team with six holes in, the smallest just large enough to take a missile and the others getting larger. Decorate the boxes if desired. Give each hole a score value, for example, one point for the largest hole, two for the next one, then five, ten, 50 and 100 (or smaller numbers depending on how many missiles you have). Give each team between 20 and 100 missiles.

Standing at a set distance, a player tries to throw their missile into another team's box. If they hit the hole, the team whose box it is must give the thrower that number of missiles. If the thrower misses, they lose the thrown missile to the other team.

Ghana: Pilolo

Designate a line that is both the starting and the finishing line. The players stand behind the line. One player hides sticks (or decorated stones, coins, or any token) at the other end of the game space. That player calls 'Pilolo!' (which means 'Time to find!'). The others run to find a hidden stick, and the first to bring their stick back across the finishing line is the winner. The game is often played with a stopwatch so that the best overall runners can be discovered.

Pakistan: Oonch neech

This is a tag game played in a space with access to sturdy things to climb on such as chairs, benches or trees. One person is 'It' and chooses either 'oonch', which is 'up' and means that being off the ground is not safe, or 'neech' which is 'down' and means that being on the ground is not safe. The first person tagged becomes 'It'.

China: The dragon

You could make a dragon's head and tail to add to the flavour of this game. Make a 'conga chain', with each person putting their hands on the shoulders or wheelchair handles of the person ahead of them. The one at the front is the dragon's head; the one at the end is the tail. The head tries to catch the tail, but the rest of the dragon's body tries to stop them. When the head eventually catches the tail, the tail becomes the head and everyone moves down a place and starts again.

Caribbean islands: Limbo

See which team can pass under a bar that gets lower each turn without touching it. With multi-age teams, you could allow both 'moving forwards while bending backwards' and 'wriggling on your tummy' styles.

Nigeria: Boat race

This is played on dry land! Mark out a winding course using whatever markers you have to hand (sticks, stones, chalk, chairs, and so on). This is the river. All the members of each team stand astride a broomstick facing backwards down the river. One team member only (the cox) faces forward. The teams race backwards down the river, guided by the cox who will need to do a lot of shouting. If you're worried that the pole might hurt someone, you could play using a stuffed pair of tights.

Indonesia: Toe stones

Lying on their backs, with bare feet, players pick up a smooth stone in their toes and throw it with their toes as far as they can down a designated course.

North America: Whirling circles

Teams of about four play together. Each team stands in a circle holding hands and runs a race up to and around one or more obstacles, keeping their circle turning all the time. If they stop whirling, they have to go back to the start.

Brazil: Rooster fight

Each player has a cloth tucked into their waistband. All stand on one foot with one arm across their chest, except those in wheelchairs who already have one arm in action to propel themselves. At the signal, each player, hopping and one-handed, tries to steal a cloth from another player, whilst avoiding having their own stolen or moving their arm or putting their other foot down. If they do, they are out, though you may wish to bend the rules to allow for younger children. The first to steal a handkerchief wins.

Healthy eating from around the world

Food is such an important part of Messy Church that it's worth tying in healthy eating with the other ideas on sport. Below are a few ideas for encouraging families to take an interest in food—the growing, preparing, cooking, presentation and eating of it. If there are people in your Messy Church from other countries, ask them for recipes or ideas.

- Have your Messy Church meal from a different country each month for a year and play music from that country as you eat
- Five-a-day: make a kebab with fruits from five different countries on it
- Mini-kebabs: make a cocktail-stick kebab with tiny items on it such as chickpeas, fresh peas, sweetcorn kernels, olives, cherry tomatoes, and so on
- Make a rainbow plate: invite everyone to make an edible rainbow with a food for each colour and to eat it all. Provide a range of fruit and vegetables in small pieces to choose from.
- Sample snacks: give families an opportunity to taste different healthy snacks that might be good alternatives at home to fatty or sugary ones
- People in many cultures pray before or after a meal: try saying grace in a different language

- Many cultures don't have a table: try eating on the floor
- Provide suitable vegetables in an unprepared state for people to peel, chop or pod and eat raw (nothing is as much fun as popping peas out of a pod)
- Have different breads from around the world to taste with a spread such as cream cheese or jam
- Grow your own: plant seeds together and bring back the produce when it's ready
- Try eating with different utensils from around the world, such as fingers, chopsticks, chapatti scoops, Thai soup spoons or scoops, 'sporks', and so on
- Make smoothies and cocktails
- Decorate buns or biscuits with flags from different countries
- Have a range of different seeds to try as sprinkles on a simple carrot salad (beware of food allergies)
- Make unsalted, unsweetened popcorn and eat it warm
- Mash berries with a potato masher and eat them
- In many parts of the world, people cook out of doors: have a campfire and cook on it, or make a traditional outdoor oven in the ground with hot stones (under supervision)
- Have a 'glutathon' cooking session: in summer or autumn invite everyone to bring in produce from their apple trees, tomato plants, vegetable plots or window boxes that are surplus to requirements. Make chutney, soup, jam or pies together.

Active prayers

Ball prayers

Pick a theme for your prayer such as people who are unwell, praises to Jesus, countries going through a hard time, thanks, streets in the community, local public buildings such as schools, pubs or council offices. Using a ball of a size that everyone of any ability can hold and throw successfully, and with the group standing in a circle, the person holding the ball calls out their short prayer, then throws the ball to someone on the other side of the circle, who then calls out their prayer and throws the ball to someone else until everyone has prayed their prayer. If someone doesn't want to pray out loud, they simply pray in silence, say 'Amen' and throw the ball as before.

For groups with a lot of younger children, over-vigorous teenagers or people with disabilities, you may prefer to sit in a circle and roll the ball to each other.

Popping prayers

Few of us can resist popping bubbles and, to be honest, this results in more laughter than heartfelt prayer. However, if you see laughter as an offering to God, you may find it a good way of motivating people to pray.

Choose a theme for prayer and, with the group sitting in a circle, invite one person or family at a time to stand in the circle and pop each bubble as the leader blows them, saying a short prayer for each bubble burst. It helps to suggest a theme for prayers each time. For example, 'Let's have the Bloggs family now. Could your prayers be thankyou prayers for different kinds of food?'

Finish with a quiet prayer along the following lines.

'The Bible tells us that a thousand years mean nothing to you, Lord. They are merely a day gone by or a few hours in the night. In your eyes, our lives last only as long as these bubbles. Thank you that you still love and value each one of us more than we can possibly imagine.' (Based on Psalm 90:4)

Goal prayers

Have a large, flat goal area made out of a net. It needs to be large enough for everyone to be able to score a goal. All over the net, leaving no gaps, attach 'targets' containing topics for prayer. The targets are large, simple images with the topic for prayer written underneath. For example:

- Thumbs up: thankyou prayers
- Thumbs down: sorry prayers
- Medicine: prayers for those who are unwell
- Hand clasping hand: prayers for local families
- Photo of town: prayers for your locality
- School: prayers for local schools
- Church: prayers for local churches

- Cross: prayers for Christians everywhere
- Messy splat logo: prayers for Messy Churches
- Government building: prayers for local MPs
- Prison bars: prayers for people in prison
- Holding hands: prayers for someone who needs God's love
- Newspaper: current news stories.

The idea is to throw or kick the ball to hit one of the targets, then for everyone to pray briefly on that topic, either out loud or silently.

Jesus Prayer jogging

This may sound irreverent, but is simply an excuse for teaching families this ancient prayer. Explain that the Jesus Prayer is very old and is prayed by monks and nuns as they sit or walk or do their work. It comes from the story of the Pharisee and the tax collector (Luke 18:9–14). The prayer is:

'Lord Jesus Christ, Son of God, have mercy on me, a sinner.'

Get families jogging on the spot at a nice slow pace and teach them the prayer to go with their breathing so that it has a rhythm.

Breathe in through your nose as you say in your head or out loud, 'Lord Jesus Christ'.

Breathe out as you say, 'Son of God'.

Breathe in as you say, 'have mercy on me'.
Breathe out as you say, 'a sinner'.

You might need to explain the words 'mercy' and 'sinner'. Then invite everyone to go for a jog round a short course, trying to keep the prayer going all the way round.

Relay prayer

Arrange each team of between three and six people around the space. Supply the teams with pens and plain pieces of card. Explain that this isn't a race as most relays are. Point out that, for a start, the teams have different numbers of people in them! Rather, it is to demonstrate something about the way that prayers, stories, faith or ideas can be handed on from one person to another throughout time or space.

Ask the first person in each team to choose what they want to pray for or about and to write or draw their subject for prayer on a card. Leaving the pens behind, this person then moves to the next member of their team, praying for the situation they've just written down. When they arrive at the second team member, they give that person the card and tell them what the prayer subject is. The second team member then sets off, praying as they go, and so on until everyone has prayed through their leg of the relay. You could repeat with a different team member devising the prayer on a different subject.

Picture prayer

Make a model or picture of the setting you want to use. In this sporty context it could be a swimming pool, a seaside, a mountain slope or a football pitch, or any other activity-based scene that has space for plenty of people in it (so a tennis match would not be a great choice as there is only a maximum of four players). Have a box of small people figures, such as the wooden ones used in reflective storytelling, PlayMobil® or Lego® figures, or use lumps of play dough to make your own.

Invite everyone to place a person in the scene.

Each person places a figure according to how he or she is feeling. For example, if someone feels life is really getting on top of them at the moment, they might place a figure out in the sea, nearly going under. If someone feels on top of the world, they might place a figure on top of a mountain, and so on.

Invite people to talk about why their figure is placed where it is and pray for each other. Don't force anyone to speak who doesn't want to, whatever age they are, as theirs might be a very sensitive situation.

You might also:

- Place a person to represent someone you would like to pray for
- Place a person to show where you'd like to be
- Place a person to show where you'd like someone else to be.

About the author

Lucy Moore gets horribly travelsick, which she can only see as God's sense of humour, as her Messy Church ministry involves a lot of travelling. Once she's arrived and recovered, her role is to introduce people to Messy Church and its support structures and encourage them that they can do it too. She works within The Bible Reading Fellowship, the home of Messy Church, with a small team of very gifted people to make the most of this wave of God's Spirit. Before working full-time with Messy Church, Lucy was a member of BRF's children's ministry team, offering training for those wanting to bring the Bible to life for children in churches and schools across the UK, and using drama and story-telling to explore the Bible with children herself.

Lucy's books include the *Messy Church* series, *The Gospels Unplugged*, *Bethlehem Carols Unplugged*, *The Lord's Prayer Unplugged*, *Colourful Creation* and *All-Age Worship*, and she presents the *Messy Church* DVD. A secondary school teacher by training, she was a Lay Canon of Portsmouth Cathedral until she moved dioceses, and enjoys acting, marvelling at the alien world of her two adult children, cheering on her husband in his work, walking Minnie the dog and reading eclectically.

A craft book with a difference! As well as bulging with craft ideas to inspire your creativity at Messy Church, it is also a journal to scribble in, doodle on and generally make your own. The intention is that it will become a scrapbook of conversations, messy moments and prayers, where you can sketch in your own ideas, list useful websites, make notes, reflect on spiritual moments, and journal your Messy Church journey.

Messy Crafts
A craft-based journal for Messy Church members
Lucy Moore
ISBN 978 0 85746 068 4   £6.99

brf.org.uk

This book sets out the theory and practice of Messy Church and offers 15 themed programme ideas to get you started, each including Bible references and background information; suggestions for ten easy-to-do creative art and craft activities; easy-to-prepare everyday recipes and family-friendly worship outlines.

Messy Church
Fresh ideas for building a Christ-centred community
Lucy Moore

ISBN 978 0 85746 145 2   £8.99

brf.org.uk

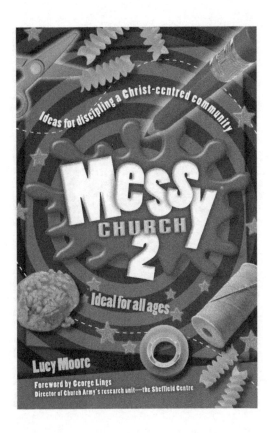

Messy Church 2 provides a further 15 exciting themed sessions and explores ways to help adults and children alike to go further and deeper with God—in other words, to grow as disciples. New to *Messy Church 2* are 'take-away' idea to help people think about their Messy Church experience between the monthly events.

Messy Church 2
Ideas for discipling a Christ-centred community
Lucy Moore
ISBN 978 0 85746 230 5   £8.99

brf.org.uk

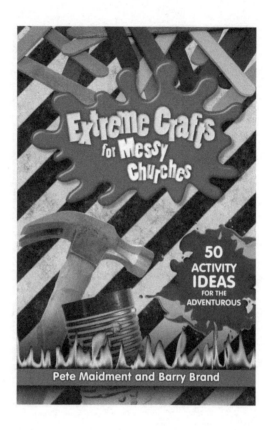

50 new activities for Messy Church sessions. Featuring Big Stuff, Construction, Science, Arty and Edible crafts, this book provides inspiration for creating a Messy Church that everyone will love to be part of.

Extreme Crafts for Messy Churches
50 activity ideas for the adventurous
Pete Maidment and Barry Brand
ISBN 978 0 85746 162 9   £7.99

brf.org.uk